PRINCEWILL LAGANG

The Science of Relationship Happiness

First published by PRINCEWILL LAGANG 2023

Copyright © 2023 by Princewill Lagang

All rights reserved. No part of this publication may be reproduced, stored or transmitted in any form or by any means, electronic, mechanical, photocopying, recording, scanning, or otherwise without written permission from the publisher. It is illegal to copy this book, post it to a website, or distribute it by any other means without permission.

Princewill Lagang asserts the moral right to be identified as the author of this work.

First edition

This book was professionally typeset on Reedsy.
Find out more at reedsy.com

Contents

1	Introduction to Relationship Happiness	1
2	The Psychology of Love and Connection	4
3	Communication: The Cornerstone of Happiness	8
4	Emotional Intelligence in Relationships	11
5	The Power of Positive Interactions	14
6	Conflict Resolution and Relationship Satisfaction	17
7	Trust and Intimacy: Pillars of Happiness	20
8	Shared Goals and Values: A Blueprint for Happiness	24
9	The Science of Physical Intimacy	27
10	Friendship and Companionship in Relationships	30
11	Managing Stress and Navigating Challenges	33
12	The Ongoing Journey of Relationship Happiness	36

1

Introduction to Relationship Happiness

In a world where connections between individuals form the fabric of society, the pursuit of happiness within relationships takes center stage. Relationships, whether romantic, familial, or platonic, play a pivotal role in our lives, shaping our emotional well-being and overall quality of life. This chapter delves into the significance of happiness within relationships and lays the foundation for a scientific exploration of the myriad factors that contribute to relationship well-being.

1.1 The Significance of Happiness in Relationships

Human beings are inherently social creatures, and the bonds we form with others contribute significantly to our overall happiness and sense of fulfillment. Relationships provide emotional support, companionship, and a sense of belonging that enrich our lives. The happiness we derive from these relationships extends beyond individual contentment, influencing the well-being of the relationship as a whole.

1.2 Defining Relationship Happiness

Relationship happiness is a multifaceted concept that encompasses emotional, psychological, and even physical satisfaction within interpersonal connections. It involves feelings of trust, intimacy, empathy, and shared joy. When individuals are content within their relationships, they are more likely to experience reduced stress levels, improved mental health, and enhanced overall life satisfaction.

1.3 Setting the Stage for Scientific Exploration

While the idea of happiness within relationships is widely acknowledged, this chapter sets the stage for a deeper examination of the scientific underpinnings of relationship well-being. Through rigorous research and empirical evidence, we will uncover the intricate factors that contribute to the maintenance and enhancement of happiness within various relationship dynamics.

1.4 The Role of Communication

Effective communication is a cornerstone of healthy relationships. It facilitates understanding, conflict resolution, and emotional connection. Scientific studies have shown that couples who communicate openly and respectfully tend to experience higher levels of relationship satisfaction. We will delve into the nuances of communication styles, active listening, and the impact of verbal and nonverbal cues on relationship happiness.

1.5 Trust and Intimacy

Trust forms the bedrock of any successful relationship. It is the foundation upon which emotional intimacy is built. Exploring the mechanisms through which trust develops, erodes, and can be rebuilt is crucial in understanding how it influences relationship happiness. Intimacy, both emotional and physical, further strengthens the bond between individuals and contributes significantly to their overall well-being.

1.6 Navigating Challenges

No relationship is immune to challenges and conflicts. How couples navigate these hurdles and work together to find solutions can significantly impact their happiness. We will explore conflict resolution strategies, the importance of empathy, and the role of compromise in maintaining relationship well-being.

1.7 The Influence of External Factors

External factors such as cultural norms, societal pressures, and economic circumstances can also influence relationship happiness. By examining how these factors intersect with individual and relational well-being, we can gain a comprehensive understanding of the complex web of influences that shape our connections with others.

1.8 The Road Ahead

As we embark on this journey to unravel the science behind relationship happiness, each subsequent chapter will delve into specific aspects of relationships, shedding light on the psychological, emotional, and social factors that contribute to the well-being of individuals and the bonds they share. By exploring the interplay between these elements, we aim to provide valuable insights into fostering and sustaining happiness within the intricate tapestry of human relationships.

2

The Psychology of Love and Connection

In the realm of relationships, the intricate dance between psychology and emotion lays the groundwork for the profound experience of love and connection. This chapter delves into the psychological underpinnings of love and attachment, highlighting how emotional connection serves as a cornerstone in the pursuit of relationship happiness.

2.1 Love and Attachment: A Psychological Exploration

Love is a complex and multifaceted emotion that has captured human attention for centuries. From the biological mechanisms that trigger attraction to the cognitive processes that deepen affection, love is deeply rooted in our psychological makeup. Attachment theory, pioneered by John Bowlby, sheds light on how our early relationships with caregivers influence our patterns of attachment in later life, shaping the way we form and maintain relationships.

2.2 The Triangular Theory of Love

Psychologist Robert Sternberg's Triangular Theory of Love breaks down love into three essential components: intimacy, passion, and commitment. Intimacy refers to the emotional closeness between individuals, passion embodies the intense physical and emotional desire, and commitment reflects the decision to maintain the relationship. Understanding how these components interact and evolve over time can offer insights into the dynamics of relationship happiness.

2.3 Emotional Connection: The Heart of Relationship Happiness

Emotional connection forms the bedrock of meaningful relationships. It involves understanding, empathy, and the ability to share vulnerabilities without fear of judgment. When individuals feel emotionally connected to their partners, they experience a sense of validation, acceptance, and security. This connection fosters a safe space where open communication and mutual support thrive.

2.4 Secure vs. Insecure Attachment Styles

Attachment styles, developed in childhood, continue to influence our relationships throughout life. Secure attachment styles are characterized by a comfortable balance between independence and reliance on others. Insecure attachment styles, such as anxious or avoidant, can hinder emotional connection and contribute to relationship conflicts. Recognizing and understanding these attachment patterns is crucial for fostering healthy emotional bonds.

2.5 Emotional Intimacy and Vulnerability

Emotional intimacy involves revealing our authentic selves to another person. This requires vulnerability—being open about our feelings, fears, and desires. When both partners are willing to be vulnerable, it creates a profound sense of closeness. Building emotional intimacy is a gradual process that requires trust and reciprocation, but the rewards are immense in terms of deepening connection and relationship satisfaction.

2.6 Cultivating Emotional Connection

Nurturing emotional connection requires intentional effort. Engaging in activities that foster shared experiences, engaging in deep conversations, and actively listening to one another can all contribute to a stronger emotional bond. Practicing empathy, validating each other's emotions, and expressing appreciation further solidify the foundation of emotional connection.

2.7 Digital Age and Emotional Connection

In the digital age, the landscape of emotional connection has expanded to include virtual interactions. However, balancing online and offline interactions is essential to maintain genuine emotional bonds. While technology can facilitate communication, it's crucial to ensure that face-to-face interactions and physical presence continue to play a significant role in cultivating emotional connection.

2.8 The Power of Rituals and Traditions

Rituals and traditions, whether simple routines or significant celebrations, play a vital role in enhancing emotional connection. These shared experiences create a sense of continuity and belonging, reinforcing the emotional ties that bind individuals together.

2.9 The Intersection of Love and Happiness

In summary, the psychology of love and connection is intrinsically linked to the pursuit of relationship happiness. Emotional connection, rooted in attachment theory, forms the bedrock of fulfilling relationships. By understanding the dynamics of emotional intimacy, recognizing attachment styles, and actively cultivating emotional connection, individuals can create a strong foundation for lasting relationship happiness. This chapter serves as a stepping stone for the exploration of practical strategies and insights to enhance emotional bonds and foster happiness within relationships.

3

Communication: The Cornerstone of Happiness

In the intricate dance of relationships, effective communication serves as the cornerstone that nurtures understanding, resolves conflicts, and fortifies emotional connection. This chapter delves into the pivotal role of communication in relationship happiness, offering insights into techniques that promote clear, respectful, and empathetic dialogue.

3.1 The Power of Communication

Communication is the lifeblood of any healthy relationship. It involves the exchange of thoughts, feelings, and ideas between individuals. Effective communication builds trust, enhances emotional intimacy, and fosters a sense of security. Conversely, poor communication can lead to misunderstandings, resentment, and deteriorating relationship quality.

3.2 Active Listening: The Key to Understanding

Active listening is a foundational communication skill that involves giving your full attention to the speaker, without interrupting or formulating responses prematurely. When individuals feel truly heard, they experience validation and connection. Practicing active listening involves maintaining eye contact, nodding to show engagement, and reflecting back what you've heard to ensure accurate understanding.

3.3 Clear and Open Expression

Expressing oneself clearly is essential for effective communication. Use "I" statements to convey your feelings and needs without placing blame. Being specific about your thoughts and emotions helps prevent misinterpretation. Avoiding assumptions and allowing room for clarification promotes mutual understanding.

3.4 Nonverbal Communication

Nonverbal cues, such as facial expressions, body language, and tone of voice, contribute significantly to the messages we convey. Being mindful of nonverbal signals is crucial to ensure that your intended message aligns with your nonverbal cues. Additionally, paying attention to your partner's nonverbal cues allows you to pick up on subtle emotions and thoughts.

3.5 Conflict Resolution Through Communication

Conflict is a natural part of any relationship. Effective communication plays a pivotal role in resolving conflicts in a healthy manner. Instead of resorting to blame or defensiveness, focus on expressing your feelings and needs while also listening to your partner's perspective. Using "I" statements, remaining calm, and practicing empathy can transform conflicts into opportunities for growth.

3.6 Empathy: The Heart of Effective Communication

Empathy is the ability to understand and share the feelings of another. It is a cornerstone of effective communication. By putting yourself in your partner's shoes and acknowledging their emotions, you create a supportive environment where they feel valued and understood. Empathetic communication fosters emotional connection and prevents misunderstandings.

3.7 Digital Communication Etiquette

In the digital age, a significant portion of communication occurs through texts, emails, and social media. It's important to uphold respectful and clear communication in these digital interactions as well. Avoid misinterpretations by using appropriate punctuation, considering the tone of your message, and being mindful of the timing and context of your communication.

3.8 Cultivating Positive Communication Habits

Cultivating positive communication habits requires conscious effort. Set aside dedicated time for meaningful conversations, free from distractions. Practice gratitude and express appreciation for your partner's efforts. Engage in light-hearted banter and humor to keep the connection playful and enjoyable.

3.9 The Reward of Effective Communication

In summary, effective communication is the bridge that connects individuals within relationships. By actively practicing techniques such as active listening, clear expression, and empathy, you can create an environment that fosters understanding, emotional intimacy, and mutual respect. This chapter serves as a guide to navigating the nuances of communication, paving the way for enhanced relationship happiness and lasting connections.

4

Emotional Intelligence in Relationships

Emotional intelligence, the ability to recognize, understand, manage, and effectively use emotions, plays a profound role in maintaining happiness and harmony within relationships. This chapter explores the significance of emotional intelligence and offers techniques for understanding and managing emotions within the context of a partnership.

4.1 The Essence of Emotional Intelligence

Emotional intelligence (EI) encompasses self-awareness, self-regulation, empathy, and social skills. It is the foundation upon which healthy relationships are built. Individuals with high EI are better equipped to navigate the complexities of emotions, both their own and their partner's, leading to improved communication, conflict resolution, and overall relationship satisfaction.

4.2 Self-Awareness: Understanding Your Emotions

Self-awareness involves recognizing and understanding your own emotions. By acknowledging your feelings, you become better equipped to manage them and prevent emotional reactions from negatively impacting your relationship. Regular self-reflection and mindfulness practices can help you become attuned to your emotional states.

4.3 Self-Regulation: Managing Your Emotions

Self-regulation refers to the ability to manage and control your emotions, particularly in challenging situations. When you can respond calmly and thoughtfully rather than reacting impulsively, you create a conducive environment for healthy communication. Breathing exercises, mindfulness, and taking breaks are techniques that aid in self-regulation.

4.4 Empathy: Understanding Your Partner's Emotions

Empathy is the cornerstone of emotional connection. It involves understanding and sharing the emotions of your partner. By putting yourself in their shoes, you gain insight into their feelings and experiences. Active listening and asking open-ended questions can help you better grasp their emotions and respond with empathy.

4.5 Social Skills: Navigating Interpersonal Dynamics

Social skills encompass effective communication, conflict resolution, and the ability to build rapport. By practicing clear communication, active listening, and assertiveness, you create an environment where both partners feel valued and understood. Conflict resolution skills help prevent misunderstandings from escalating into larger issues.

4.6 Emotional Intelligence and Relationship Happiness

Couples with high emotional intelligence tend to experience greater relationship satisfaction. The ability to understand and manage emotions promotes healthier interactions and reduces the risk of misunderstandings. Partners who exhibit empathy and actively practice emotional intelligence create a nurturing and supportive environment.

4.7 Techniques for Enhancing Emotional Intelligence

- Emotion Journaling: Keep a journal to track your emotions, triggers, and reactions. This practice fosters self-awareness and helps you identify patterns in your emotional responses.

- Mindfulness Meditation: Engage in mindfulness practices to stay present and connected with your emotions. Mindfulness enhances self-regulation and helps you respond rather than react impulsively.

- Role Reversal: Practice empathy by imagining yourself in your partner's situation. This helps you understand their emotions more deeply and respond with compassion.

- Conflict De-escalation: During conflicts, take breaks if emotions run high. Engage in self-soothing techniques and return to the conversation when both partners are calmer and more open to understanding each other.

- Emotional Check-Ins: Regularly check in with your partner about their emotional state. This encourages open communication and provides opportunities to address any concerns promptly.

4.8 A Journey of Growth

In summary, emotional intelligence serves as a guiding light in nurturing healthy and fulfilling relationships. By cultivating self-awareness, self-regulation, empathy, and social skills, you pave the way for effective communication, understanding, and lasting happiness. This chapter emphasizes the importance of emotional intelligence as a journey of growth, leading to stronger emotional bonds and enriched relationships.

5

The Power of Positive Interactions

In the realm of relationships, the power of positive interactions cannot be underestimated. These interactions serve as the building blocks of happiness, creating a foundation of warmth, connection, and shared joy. This chapter explores the significance of positive interactions and offers techniques for fostering positivity and gratitude within the relationship.

5.1 The Magic of Positive Interactions

Positive interactions encompass acts of kindness, affection, appreciation, and shared laughter. These moments contribute to the emotional bank account of a relationship, enhancing overall well-being and relationship satisfaction. Positive interactions create a reservoir of goodwill that buffers against the inevitable challenges that relationships face.

5.2 The Ripple Effect of Positivity

Positive interactions create a ripple effect that extends beyond the moment. A kind word, a heartfelt gesture, or a shared laugh can uplift both partners' moods and set a positive tone for the relationship. The accumulation of these interactions over time creates a positive atmosphere where both partners feel valued and cherished.

5.3 The Importance of Gratitude

Gratitude is a powerful emotion that fuels positive interactions. Expressing appreciation for your partner's efforts and qualities fosters a sense of validation and acknowledgment. Regular expressions of gratitude contribute to a culture of positivity within the relationship.

5.4 Techniques for Fostering Positivity

- Random Acts of Kindness: Surprise your partner with thoughtful gestures, whether it's making their favorite meal or leaving a heartfelt note. These acts of kindness show your appreciation and create moments of shared happiness.

- Compliments: Compliment your partner sincerely and frequently. Recognize their achievements and qualities, reinforcing their self-esteem and the positivity within the relationship.

- Shared Experiences: Engage in activities that bring joy and laughter. Shared experiences like watching a movie, going for a walk, or trying a new hobby create lasting memories of happiness.

- Quality Time: Dedicate meaningful time to connect without distractions. Engage in deep conversations, reminisce about positive memories, and strengthen your emotional bond.

- Appreciation Rituals: Establish rituals like a weekly gratitude session where you both share things you appreciate about each other. This practice reinforces positive interactions and enhances the overall atmosphere of the relationship.

5.5 Overcoming Negativity Bias

Humans have a natural tendency to focus on negative experiences. Counteract this bias by intentionally focusing on positive interactions. When disagreements or conflicts arise, consciously remind yourselves of the positive interactions you've shared to maintain a balanced perspective.

5.6 Building a Positive Mindset

Cultivating a positive mindset is an ongoing practice. Engage in self-care to ensure your own emotional well-being, as your mood significantly impacts the relationship's atmosphere. By nurturing your own positivity, you contribute to a healthier emotional climate for both partners.

5.7 The Butterfly Effect of Happiness

In summary, positive interactions serve as the glue that holds relationships together. Their impact extends far beyond the moment, shaping the emotional landscape of the partnership. By practicing kindness, expressing gratitude, and intentionally fostering positivity, you contribute to a cycle of happiness that enhances the overall quality of your relationship. This chapter underscores the transformative power of positive interactions and offers techniques to infuse your relationship with joy, appreciation, and lasting happiness.

6

Conflict Resolution and Relationship Satisfaction

Within the tapestry of relationships, conflicts are inevitable. However, the way conflicts are managed plays a crucial role in determining the overall happiness and satisfaction within the partnership. This chapter delves into the connection between conflict resolution and relationship happiness, offering strategies for resolving conflicts constructively and nurturing satisfaction.

6.1 The Dynamics of Conflict

Conflicts arise from differences in perspectives, needs, and expectations. How these conflicts are addressed can either strengthen the relationship or create rifts. Addressing conflicts in a healthy manner is key to maintaining the emotional well-being of both partners.

6.2 The Link Between Conflict Resolution and Happiness

Conflict resolution is intimately tied to relationship satisfaction. Partners who are adept at resolving conflicts in a respectful and empathetic manner experience higher levels of trust, emotional intimacy, and overall happiness. Constructive conflict resolution promotes growth, understanding, and mutual respect.

6.3 Strategies for Constructive Conflict Resolution

- Calm Communication: Approach conflicts when both partners are calm and willing to engage. Use "I" statements to express your feelings and avoid blame.

- Active Listening: Listen attentively to your partner's perspective without interrupting. This demonstrates respect and sets the stage for a productive dialogue.

- Empathy: Put yourself in your partner's shoes and acknowledge their emotions. This validates their feelings and creates a safe space for discussion.

- Seek Common Ground: Focus on finding solutions that are mutually beneficial. Look for areas of compromise and collaborate to address the underlying issues.

- Time-Outs: If emotions run high, take a break to cool off before continuing the discussion. This prevents heated arguments and allows for more rational communication.

6.4 The Role of Emotional Regulation

Emotional regulation is crucial during conflicts. Being aware of your emotional state and managing your reactions prevent escalations and maintain a productive atmosphere. Techniques like deep breathing, counting to ten, or engaging in physical activity can help manage intense emotions.

6.5 Healthy Conflict vs. Destructive Conflict

Healthy conflict is characterized by respectful communication, willingness to understand, and a focus on finding solutions. Destructive conflict involves insults, blame, and personal attacks. Differentiating between the two and striving for healthy conflict resolution is essential for relationship satisfaction.

6.6 Seeking Professional Help

In cases where conflicts persist and solutions seem elusive, seeking the guidance of a couples' therapist can be invaluable. A trained professional can facilitate productive communication, offer insights, and provide tools for resolving conflicts more effectively.

6.7 Post-Conflict Reconnection

After conflicts are resolved, it's essential to reconnect and reaffirm your emotional bond. Engage in positive interactions, express gratitude for working through the conflict, and assure your partner of your commitment to the relationship.

6.8 The Path to Lasting Happiness

In summary, conflict resolution is an integral part of maintaining a happy and satisfying relationship. By approaching conflicts with empathy, active listening, and a focus on resolution, you pave the way for emotional growth and increased understanding. Constructive conflict resolution promotes a positive emotional climate and contributes to the overall happiness and well-being of both partners. This chapter highlights the importance of navigating conflicts with care and offers strategies for fostering lasting happiness within the relationship.

7

Trust and Intimacy: Pillars of Happiness

In the intricate landscape of relationships, trust and intimacy stand as pillars that support the foundation of happiness. This chapter delves into the profound relationship between trust, intimacy, and happiness within partnerships. It also offers techniques for building and maintaining these essential elements that contribute to a fulfilling and joyful relationship.

7.1 Trust: The Cornerstone of Connection

Trust is the bedrock upon which relationships are built. It involves relying on your partner's honesty, reliability, and integrity. Trust fosters a sense of security and emotional safety, allowing individuals to open up, express themselves, and engage in vulnerable conversations.

7.2 Intimacy: The Heartbeat of Emotional Bonding

Intimacy goes beyond physical closeness. Emotional intimacy involves sharing one's deepest thoughts, fears, and desires with a partner. It is nurtured through open communication, empathy, and a willingness to be vulnerable. Intimacy deepens the connection between partners and enhances the overall quality of the relationship.

7.3 The Interplay Between Trust, Intimacy, and Happiness

Trust and intimacy are intrinsically linked to happiness within relationships. A foundation of trust allows partners to feel secure and confident in their emotional bond. Intimacy, on the other hand, creates a space where partners can be their authentic selves and experience genuine connection. Together, these elements form the basis for emotional well-being and relationship satisfaction.

7.4 Building Trust

- Consistency: Fulfill promises and commitments consistently to establish reliability.

- Open Communication: Share your thoughts, feelings, and intentions openly and honestly.

- Transparency: Be transparent about your actions and decisions, especially when they impact the relationship.

- Boundaries: Respect each other's boundaries to create a sense of safety and comfort.

7.5 Nurturing Intimacy

- Emotional Sharing: Share your dreams, fears, and aspirations to create a sense of emotional closeness.

- Active Listening: Listen attentively when your partner shares their thoughts and feelings, showing that you value their perspective.

- Quality Time: Dedicate focused and uninterrupted time for deep conversations and shared experiences.

- Physical Touch: Physical affection, such as hugs, kisses, and cuddling, reinforces emotional connection.

7.6 Overcoming Trust Issues

If trust has been compromised in the past, rebuilding it requires patience and effort. Open communication, consistent actions, and forgiveness play key roles in healing and rebuilding trust.

7.7 Fostering Intimacy Over Time

Maintaining intimacy over the long term requires ongoing effort. Continue to explore each other's thoughts and feelings, try new activities together, and keep the lines of communication open.

7.8 Seeking Professional Help

In cases where trust and intimacy issues are deeply rooted or challenging to navigate, seeking the guidance of a therapist can be beneficial. A therapist can provide tools and insights to address trust and intimacy concerns effectively.

7.9 The Art of Balancing

In summary, trust and intimacy are the pillars that uphold the happiness and fulfillment of a relationship. Building and nurturing these elements require a delicate balance of vulnerability, communication, and mutual respect. By cultivating trust and fostering intimacy, you create a strong emotional foundation that supports lasting happiness and strengthens the bonds between partners. This chapter underscores the vital role of trust and intimacy in relationship satisfaction and offers techniques to cultivate and maintain these essential elements.

8

Shared Goals and Values: A Blueprint for Happiness

In the tapestry of relationships, shared goals and values serve as a guiding compass that steers the journey toward lasting happiness. This chapter delves into the profound impact of shared goals and values on relationship happiness. It also offers strategies for aligning aspirations and creating a shared vision that nurtures a strong and harmonious partnership.

8.1 The Significance of Shared Goals and Values

Shared goals and values form the basis of a shared life. They offer direction, purpose, and a sense of unity within the relationship. Partners who align their aspirations and values are more likely to experience a deeper connection, enhanced communication, and a stronger bond.

8.2 Creating a Shared Vision

A shared vision involves envisioning the future you both desire together. This could encompass career aspirations, family planning, financial goals, and personal growth. A shared vision acts as a roadmap that guides decisions, strengthens resolve during challenges, and cultivates a sense of togetherness.

8.3 Impact on Relationship Satisfaction

Couples with aligned goals and values experience higher levels of relationship satisfaction. Having a common purpose fosters a sense of teamwork and mutual support. The shared journey toward common goals enhances emotional intimacy and strengthens the emotional bond.

8.4 Strategies for Aligning Goals and Values

- Open Dialogue: Engage in conversations about your individual goals, dreams, and values. Explore where your aspirations overlap and where differences arise.

- Active Listening: Listen carefully to your partner's aspirations and values, seeking to understand their perspective and motivations.

- Compromise: In cases where there are differences, strive to find compromises that honor both partners' needs and values.

- Prioritize Communication: Continuously communicate about your shared goals and vision. Revisit these conversations regularly to ensure you remain on the same page.

8.5 Balancing Individuality and Togetherness

While shared goals are important, it's also crucial to maintain individual identities and pursuits. Balancing personal growth and the shared journey contributes to a well-rounded and harmonious relationship.

8.6 Reassessing and Realigning

As life evolves, so do aspirations and values. Regularly reassess and realign your shared goals and vision. This keeps the partnership dynamic and ensures that your journey remains congruent with both partners' changing aspirations.

8.7 Overcoming Differences

In cases where significant differences in goals and values arise, open and honest communication is vital. Seek to understand each other's perspectives and explore potential compromises that align with both partners' core values.

8.8 Seeking Professional Guidance

If challenges arise in aligning goals and values, a couples' therapist can provide guidance. Therapists can facilitate discussions, offer insights, and provide strategies for finding common ground.

8.9 The Tapestry of Happiness

In summary, shared goals and values create a strong foundation for happiness within relationships. A shared vision offers purpose and unity, enhancing the emotional connection and overall satisfaction. By aligning aspirations, fostering open communication, and prioritizing compromise, you weave a tapestry of shared happiness that withstands the test of time. This chapter underscores the transformative power of shared goals and values and provides strategies to cultivate a partnership enriched by a shared journey toward lasting happiness.

9

The Science of Physical Intimacy

In the intricate dance of relationships, physical intimacy serves as a powerful means of deepening connection and fostering happiness. This chapter delves into the science behind physical intimacy and its role in building a strong emotional bond. It also offers techniques for enhancing physical intimacy to enrich the overall happiness within the partnership.

9.1 The Biological and Psychological Significance

Physical intimacy triggers a cascade of biological and psychological reactions that contribute to emotional closeness. Touch, hugs, kisses, and sexual activity stimulate the release of oxytocin and endorphins—hormones associated with bonding, pleasure, and reduced stress.

9.2 The Emotional Connection

Physical intimacy enhances emotional connection by fostering a sense of safety, trust, and vulnerability. Intimate touch and closeness create a unique language that communicates affection, desire, and love without words.

9.3 Enhancing Physical Intimacy

- Open Communication: Discuss your preferences, boundaries, and desires openly with your partner. Communication is essential for understanding each other's needs and ensuring both partners are comfortable.

- Quality Time: Dedicate time to physical closeness without the expectation of sexual activity. Cuddling, holding hands, and sharing a quiet moment can be just as meaningful as sexual intimacy.

- Variety and Exploration: Be open to trying new experiences and exploring different forms of physical intimacy that align with both partners' comfort levels.

- Empathy: Tune into your partner's signals and responses during physical intimacy. Being attuned to their comfort and enjoyment enhances the experience for both.

9.4 The Role of Trust and Consent

Physical intimacy is built on a foundation of trust and consent. It's crucial to prioritize your partner's boundaries and ensure that both partners are on the same page. Respect for each other's comfort zones creates an environment where physical intimacy can thrive.

9.5 Intimacy Beyond Sex

Physical intimacy extends beyond sexual activity. Non-sexual physical touch, such as hugs, kisses, and cuddling, can strengthen the emotional bond. Intimacy can also be expressed through gestures like holding hands, brushing hair, or offering a massage.

9.6 Intimacy Challenges

Physical intimacy can be influenced by factors such as stress, health issues, and life changes. Open communication about these challenges is essential. Seek understanding, offer support, and explore ways to adapt physical intimacy to changing circumstances.

9.7 Emotional Aftercare

After intimate moments, prioritize emotional aftercare. This involves offering comfort, reassurance, and a sense of closeness. Emotional connection and communication in the aftermath of physical intimacy strengthen the overall bond.

9.8 A Path to Deepened Connection

In summary, physical intimacy is a powerful tool for deepening emotional connection within relationships. By understanding the biological and emotional significance, practicing open communication, and prioritizing consent and trust, you create an environment where physical intimacy thrives. Intimacy, whether sexual or non-sexual, contributes to a sense of closeness, pleasure, and overall happiness within the partnership. This chapter underscores the role of physical intimacy in the journey to lasting happiness and offers techniques to enhance the physical dimension of your emotional bond.

10

Friendship and Companionship in Relationships

In the intricate fabric of relationships, friendship and companionship serve as the threads that weave together moments of joy, understanding, and shared experiences. This chapter delves into the profound significance of friendship within romantic partnerships and offers techniques for fostering companionship and cultivating shared interests, enriching the tapestry of relationship happiness.

10.1 The Role of Friendship in Relationships

Friendship forms the foundation upon which romantic relationships thrive. Beyond romantic attraction, the bond of friendship offers a sense of comfort, trust, and a deep understanding of each other's personalities and quirks. Friends who are also romantic partners tend to experience heightened relationship satisfaction.

10.2 Nurturing Companionship

Companionship involves enjoying each other's company, engaging in activities together, and sharing moments of laughter and relaxation. Cultivating companionship ensures that the partnership is grounded in shared experiences and mutual enjoyment.

10.3 Techniques for Fostering Companionship

- Shared Interests: Discover and explore activities you both enjoy. Whether it's a shared hobby, a TV show, or a favorite type of cuisine, common interests provide opportunities for bonding.

- Quality Time: Dedicate regular time for one-on-one interaction. Engage in conversations, go for walks, or simply spend time relaxing together.

- Playfulness: Embrace a spirit of playfulness and lightheartedness. Engage in activities that make you both laugh and create moments of shared joy.

- Supportive Conversations: Discuss each other's goals, dreams, and challenges. Offering emotional support and encouragement nurtures a sense of companionship and shared growth.

10.4 The Importance of Communication

Communication is essential for cultivating companionship. Share your thoughts, feelings, and experiences openly. Engage in meaningful conversations that go beyond day-to-day matters to strengthen your emotional bond.

10.5 Balancing Individuality and Togetherness

While companionship is vital, maintaining individuality is equally important. Allow each other space to pursue individual interests and friendships. Balancing togetherness with personal growth ensures a well-rounded and healthy relationship.

10.6 Building New Experiences

Continuously seek opportunities to build new experiences together. Travel to new places, try new activities, and step out of your comfort zones to create a treasury of shared memories.

10.7 Overcoming Routine

As relationships mature, routines can become more established. While routines offer stability, they can also lead to predictability. Introduce variety and spontaneity to keep the companionship fresh and exciting.

10.8 The Journey of Friendship

In summary, friendship and companionship form the cornerstone of relationship happiness. By nurturing shared interests, engaging in meaningful conversations, and cultivating a sense of playfulness, you strengthen the bond that transcends romantic attraction. The journey of friendship within a romantic partnership creates a tapestry of shared memories, mutual support, and lasting joy. This chapter underscores the importance of friendship and companionship in the pursuit of happiness within relationships and offers techniques to deepen these essential aspects of your partnership.

11

Managing Stress and Navigating Challenges

Within the intricate tapestry of relationships, stress and challenges are inevitable threads. This chapter delves into the impact of stress on relationship happiness and well-being, offering strategies for managing stress together and thriving in the face of challenges.

11.1 The Interplay of Stress and Relationships

Stress can cast a shadow over relationship happiness. External pressures, work-related demands, and personal challenges can impact both partners' emotional states and strain the partnership. However, how couples navigate stress can determine the strength of their emotional bond.

11.2 The Importance of Teamwork

Facing stress as a united team strengthens the partnership. When both partners support each other, share responsibilities, and collaborate to address challenges, the emotional bond deepens and the impact of stress is mitigated.

11.3 Strategies for Managing Stress Together

- Open Communication: Discuss your stressors, concerns, and feelings openly. Sharing your experiences allows your partner to understand your perspective and provide support.

- Active Listening: Listen attentively when your partner expresses their stressors. Offer empathy, validation, and a willingness to help.

- Shared Problem-Solving: Collaborate to find solutions to shared stressors. Brainstorm ideas, make joint decisions, and work together to alleviate challenges.

- Emotional Support: Offer emotional support by validating your partner's feelings and providing reassurance. Expressing your love and commitment can alleviate feelings of isolation.

11.4 Practicing Self-Care

Individual self-care is vital for managing stress within the relationship. When both partners prioritize their well-being, they are better equipped to navigate stressors together. Engage in activities that promote relaxation, exercise, and emotional well-being.

11.5 Balancing Support and Independence

While supporting each other is crucial, maintaining individual independence is equally important. Balance emotional support with respecting each other's space and autonomy.

11.6 Seeking Professional Help

In cases where stressors become overwhelming or chronic, seeking the guidance of a therapist can be beneficial. Therapists can offer coping strategies, communication tools, and insights to navigate challenges more effectively.

11.7 Cultivating Resilience

Resilience involves the ability to bounce back from challenges. By facing stressors as a team and seeking growth opportunities within challenges, you cultivate resilience that strengthens your partnership.

11.8 The Strength of Unity

In summary, managing stress and navigating challenges as a team enhances the emotional bond and overall relationship happiness. By practicing open communication, offering mutual support, and prioritizing self-care, you create a resilient partnership that thrives in the face of adversity. The unity forged through shared challenges becomes a testament to the strength of your emotional connection. This chapter underscores the transformative power of teamwork in managing stress and offers strategies to navigate challenges while nurturing your relationship's well-being and happiness.

12

The Ongoing Journey of Relationship Happiness

As we reach the culmination of this exploration, it's essential to reflect on the science-backed practices that form the tapestry of relationship happiness. This chapter embraces the concept of an ongoing journey, offering insights into nurturing a culture of growth, connection, and joy that sustains the happiness within the partnership.

12.1 Embracing the Lessons

Throughout this journey, we've delved into the significance of various aspects that contribute to relationship happiness: communication, emotional intelligence, trust, intimacy, shared goals, and more. Each chapter has offered techniques rooted in science to enhance these elements. Reflecting on these lessons allows you to weave them into the fabric of your partnership.

12.2 Navigating Evolving Dynamics

Relationships are dynamic and ever-evolving. What works at one stage may need adjustment at another. As life circumstances change, continue to adapt the techniques and strategies to fit your current context, fostering a relationship that remains relevant and fulfilling.

12.3 The Essence of Connection

At the heart of this ongoing journey is the essence of connection. Continuously prioritize open communication, understanding, and mutual respect. Make time for quality interactions that reinforce emotional bonds and strengthen the connection between partners.

12.4 Embracing Growth

Relationships are a fertile ground for personal and joint growth. Approach challenges as opportunities for learning and development. Embrace change, celebrate milestones, and evolve together as individuals and as a partnership.

12.5 The Gift of Shared Memories

Create a treasury of shared memories. Engage in new experiences, revisit fond moments, and continue to build a collection of stories that illustrate the journey you've undertaken together.

12.6 The Power of Appreciation

Never underestimate the power of appreciation. Express gratitude for your partner's presence, efforts, and the happiness they bring to your life. Regularly reflect on the positive aspects of your relationship and acknowledge them openly.

12.7 Cultivating Joy

Infuse joy into your relationship. Engage in activities that make you both laugh, explore new interests together, and create an atmosphere that radiates positivity.

12.8 Seeking Professional Support

In times of uncertainty or challenge, seeking professional guidance is a sign of strength, not weakness. Therapists can offer insights, communication tools, and strategies to navigate complexities and maintain relationship happiness.

12.9 An Ever-Growing Tapestry

In summary, the journey of relationship happiness is an ever-growing tapestry woven with the threads of communication, emotional connection, shared experiences, and mutual support. By embracing the lessons learned, adapting to change, and nurturing growth and joy, you create a relationship that evolves, deepens, and flourishes over time.

12.10 Your Unique Journey

Your journey is uniquely yours. The science-backed practices offered in this exploration provide a foundation, but the path you tread is guided by your individual dynamics, aspirations, and love. As you continue forward, remember that the journey of relationship happiness is ongoing—an adventure filled with shared moments, challenges conquered, and a love that grows stronger with each step.

www.ingramcontent.com/pod-product-compliance
Lightning Source LLC
LaVergne TN
LVHW020739090526
838202LV00057BA/5987